T0194186

Beautifully Sinful Lips

J. Pushkarna

authorHOUSE®

AuthorHouse™
1663 Liberty Drive
Bloomington, IN 47403
www.authorhouse.com
Phone: 1 (800) 839-8640

Published by AuthorHouse 02/04/2020

ISBN: 978-1-7283-4613-7 (sc)
ISBN: 978-1-7283-4611-3 (hc)
ISBN: 978-1-7283-4612-0 (e)

Library of Congress Control Number: 2020902347

Print information available on the last page.

This book is printed on acid-free paper.

Even the devil liked the taste of her

He would always cum while he ate her

I can't tell the truth
I have to look at many
And lie
I say I'm ok
When I'm drowning
Doesn't anybody see
I grew
The demons
Well they changed me
Don't worry I'll be the one laughing
I'm not giving up
I can handle the pain
I can handle the stares
I'm covered in a story
I told
Stop staring at me
Men fucked me up
When they thought they would own me
Not a father brother husband or friend
Can tell me
You don't want my opinion
Life changed me
I'm no longer innocent
Sex made me
Broke me
I fixed me
I made many mistakes
Silencing myself
For the sake of hurting others
You all deserve the truth
Your mistakes aren't on me
Truth is you can't face honesty
So in a world of lies
One more lie won't hurt

Too opinionated
She is just too much
Not enough
She is what others think of her
Her words are poetic
They don't need to believe
Just wait and see
Is all she is thinking
The world we live in
Still shames you
Just for being you
So smile through the pain
Stand with grace
Be too opinionated
It's what will get you to the good days
Don't back down
Don't save face
If they don't like what you have to say
Then they don't belong
Don't sit with the two faced
It's a mistake
This world has deemed you unfit
Too much
And not enough
It's okay to say no
With no explanation
This isn't how it works
Anymore

The girl in the mirror is back
She is quite taunting tonight
Not her usual self
I see a smirk on her beautiful face
I can't help but wonder
What game is she trying to play?
I see her from time to time
But tonight
She doesn't want to leave
I wonder if I should ask her
Who is she trying to deceive?
I know she knows the question
And has the answer to what I'm about to say
If I smash the glass
Maybe then she'll go away
I sometimes cover all the mirrors
In the house
Afraid if I look what will I actually see
But tonight oh tonight
She is taunting me.

She sinned
So beautifully
The devil
Knew he couldn't win

Beautifully sinful lips
She was silenced by the opinion of others
Fearful of who she would offend
What will she regret when her time comes to an end?
Will she regret not telling people?
All that her sinful eyes do see
Women being shamed
For who they were born to be
How cruel the world can be
To a young mother of three
How those tattoos on your skin
Tell a story
Of irony
Of living in fear
They judged her
She stayed silent
Would they doom her too much?
Too loud
Or maybe she isn't enough in a world of centerfold girls
Maybe the world wants her opinion
In a sinful way she fed the wolves her body
Only for them to call her names of disgrace
Cause her skirt was too short
Or she caught onto their games
In a beautiful world
She was cursed
With sinful lips
Luscious not pure
How do I tell her?
Silence isn't strength
And her beauty isn't a shame
Her words not a waste
Oh beauty
It's not a sin.

What is a sinner's game?
Don't ever believe what they say
Their words will hypnotize you
They share no morals
Their values are never the same
They believed they are justified
In their rights to your name
When they look in the mirror
They see a white knight
They don't see a bad guy
A dominating sex god
Is all they see
They have rights to your body
Since that one romantic night
When you didn't see their true face
The sinners game
He has to play no more
He shames you for the makeup you wear
All your friends are whores
Not you baby
You're as pure as can be
That's how he controls you, can't you see?
There is a problem with him
Not you hunny
It's his lies
Not yours
His games are well played
He's a sinner
Disguised as a saint

All I've known is pain
Because I choose to feel the hurt
I've seen beauty
But I've felt true real pain
It aches
I'll tell you now it felt like blades
Cutting deep in my soul
Slowly taking pieces of me away
I stood tall through it all
With blood running down my body
I felt that pain
I didn't run or even crawl
I didn't even lay down
I may though have let it consume me
Cause through it all
I only saw a different ending
I saw a different me
Slowly I did get up from that girl
And left her there to let her bleed
Through all her hurt, pain and suffering
I couldn't be with her you see
Cause when I finally left her
I found me.

I dream of death
And when I wake
I am living.

I didn't do it on purpose, I did it to protect myself you see!
I did it to build boundaries
To separate myself so no one could see
All the pain I had hidden
Deep within me
When I was hurting and alone
I felt my tears hit the floor
They shattered like glass
Now I stand here before you
Trying to let you see
The real me
The girl I was before the pain
The girl I was before life changed me
Now I stand here
Trying to breathe
Cause I gave you the knife
And as much as I believe in us
I'm still waiting to see if you cut me
As I wait, I wonder will it be deep
I hope if you do it's the final stabbing I need to end me for eternity
Cause this wall I built is coming down
I'm scared and afraid
But I hope you see
I'm making myself vulnerable
Cause I fell in love with a man
And I handed him the knife.

Men
I've had few
I know what they can do
They can, without a thought
Teach you a lesson
You were too young to learn
With age comes knowledge
And now I know
It's too late
The damage has been done!

I live in the shadows
I visit you in your sleep
I haunt you from your core
You wish you would hear me no more
You keep coming back
I stole years from you
Days from you
I make your nightmares a reality
Yet you still come back
You've always feared what I would do
Now look at you
You think you're crazy
You think you're lost
Completely consumed by me
You can't escape me
Cause you're the one that calls me baby
My features are pretty
And you want more
You wish to taste me
Your hunger never quite satisfied
I keep you begging
Now I know you're the one wishing
You didn't open the door

.

Light flickers all around
The smell of your cigarette lingers
Your cologne so strong, I can almost taste it
My knees get weak when you touch me
I fear the day I wake up without you
The thought of you consumes me
Can this be real?
I promised myself never again
Can you save me from the inevitable end?
I tend to go all in
Way too soon
Before I even know the real you
Why do I give you so much of me?
I know these men don't really love me
Before I can say no we're at it again
I can't handle another one leaving
I can't handle asking why anymore
As you act like a ghost as you walk out the door
I don't understand
Aren't we all looking for the same thing?
Someone to bear our truths too
If you're just going to leave
Why did you act like you wanted to save me?
Don't worry it's okay just go
You knew from the beginning I wasn't the one
But still you lead me on
Falling in love with an unwritten song
The lyrics are playing in my head
So now I really know
I have to go.
I won't say goodbye
After all, the only thing these men taught me was how to lie
I'll just destroy it before it can come true
In reality there was never a chance for me and you

He's back again today
The shadow man
He's in the corner
Waiting for the world to break me
Life's demands are tasking on me
I feel the weight
It's heavy on my shoulders
His teeth are ready
To sink into my soul
He wants me to fail
But I won't let him win
I'm on the floor again
Asking god to free me of my sins
I did what I had to
In a world of less clothes
And more skin
I showed my cleavage
For a couple more likes
Even put a smile
That, at home I hide
I let people believe that I'm happier
Than what they see
The world is rotten
And I muse
A puppet I am now
With no moral legs
This man I see
Is no man to me
He claims he is my conscience
And nothing more
A couple men DM me, telling me again I'm a whore
I want the world to be a better place
But there is no world anymore.

When you opened the door and let the devil in
Were you surprised that he wanted to play?
Oh baby, come here
You're high off the pain
So he gives you some more
A little taste
He's already taken your life away
When you wake on the floor
Still hurting from the night before
I promise I'll have more
Please don't try and stray like you did before
Cause every time I came knocking, you opened the door
I know you'll try to run and hide
You're a liar and nothing more
I'm all you have and now you want to stray
Fuck the tears
You're hooked on me
I'll take the pain away, stop begging it's not becoming
Do you feel the anger and hurt?
Is that rage I'm sensing?
You're lying to yourself
If you think this time you'll succeed at quitting me
Yesterday I had you begging on your knees
Now you have a conscience
Baby please
I'm the drug and you're the fien.

I begged and prayed to god
For many things
Some of my blessings I know are from above
I've asked the universe to take some people out of my life
The world moved me
I'm lonely
I live in fear
I've looked darkness in the face
It's evil
Just to be clear
Many of the things I've asked for I've received
I've trusted many manipulators
And put hope in lies
Sometimes I wonder why
I still pray for those who have disgraced me
I believe in life, I've created it
I have a gut feeling to trust few
I know I have been betrayed
From those who have seen my tears
But I still kept their secrets
It's not fair
I'll continue to smile
Cause I'll be damned if bitch you break me
You don't have that kind of power
The devil himself has asked me how
He handed me the knife to end my pain
Just know I thought twice
He stays in the shadows & lingers in the air
I'm on my knees again asking god to answer my prayers
Cause some of this strength, I've never felt before
I know it's him trying to save me
This life can sometimes be amazing
Just hold on one day more
The girl in the mirror is back

And this time she is waving
Calling me home I assume
I hear the devil whisper baby you're doomed
I wish to bleed these issues out of me
The voices want to play
I try so hard to keep them at bay
If I could give in
I would
But I know I have to fight'
I won't say hi to her tonight
She brings me closer to him
So tonight I'll fall to the floor on my knees
And beg God for something more
Than a life of grief with these emotional thieves.

Take my hand
Grip it tight
The bridge is wobbly tonight
My gut is screaming no don't go!
You don't know what lays ahead
It looks cold and dark
I am hesitant
I am shaking
It feels familiar
I know I'm not the same anymore
Her hand in mine
Was she walking me to our grave?
But wait, when did this happen?
I never saw a white light
You won't
I turn to see the man who answered me
His horns are long and his eyes are red
You committed a moral sin
When you crossed that bridge
Now it's time
To come with me
You sold your soul baby
Now his hooves are clacking and she let go
My legs feel heavy
I can hear my mom scream no not my baby!
What is that loud clatter?
It's the dirt hitting you
Why didn't anyone stop?
He said, she tried but you wouldn't listen
Now God is nowhere to be found
And it's just me cold in the ground
Cause this time when he handed me the knife
I wanted the pain to go away
To finally be free
I felt the evil bleed out of me.

She couldn't see a future where she existed
Together we made a deal
Now I carry her with me
She stays in the dark place
She's the one who stared our demons in their face
Her strength and courage
Got me to this place
I still see her in the mirror from to time to time
Always a simple hello and hard goodbye.

Sometimes I wish you didn't trigger me
Just the very thought of you
Feels like a knife inside of me
My past is my fear
Will I let that woman take over me?
See, the old me and the new
Aren't the same me
I once flinched at a simple touch
Or would spend my nights awake
Pretending to be asleep
When he comes home this time will he kill me?
After years it becomes a game
Can I finally get him to end my pain?
You see no way out
The road needs to end
And if I let him kill me
The devil will take my hand
And bring me home
Cause at this point you don't believe in a God
Even when you fall to your knees and pray
The 1-800 help lines know your name
But not a single soul knows your shame
My kids saw it again
I thought I was going to be able to take all the blame
But here I am triggered by my mistakes
Cause I fucking stayed
And when I got away
The old me lied and told me to go back
I needed my fix
Who am I really without all of this?

My daily fight is waking up
Just that feeling every day I have to force my eyes open
They want to stay shut
They don't feel as heavy
If I keep them closed my reality doesn't bite me
I don't feel the pain of loneliness
I don't feel the world's demands
The world isn't spinning with expectations
For me to be a certain person
A happy grateful mom
A woman who's empowered by her body
A woman who isn't exhausted
My truth
The pressures to be something, I'm not
Aren't there when my eyes are closed
Lately I feel as if I've lost the fight
If my will to be grateful has left my present
The world is making me cold
And when my eyes are sleepy and closed tight
I feel serenity.

I can handle my demons she repeated to herself
As she stared at her reflection
We can handle them
It's time to put them back in their place
Some days they take over
And scream in my face
Her reflection answered, "I know"
She heard a voice
She stood there dumb founded
They were answering
They said, "some days you don't seem to hear us anymore"
She stared and said
"I can hear you always, I carry you with me
Just know I don't listen"
Your voice isn't in control
She stared and said, "I am"
With a bow and nod
She walked away
"Not today" she said "not anymore" she repeated
I am stronger than you
I will fight you and win
I will fight you and I will win.

Please don't let him be your demise
You opened the door and let him in
That doesn't mean he wins
You can take back what's yours
You control the ending
You don't need to fall for him
His smile
His eyes
All those beautiful lies
Are what's killing you inside
Let go of what was
Look at what is
And stop saying you're crazy
This isn't about pride
Put all the anger and hate aside
Breathe in & out
Don't sacrifice another thing
For the thought of a life filled with lies
It isn't love beautiful
Love doesn't take what you've built and try to break the walls of protection
for self-validation
Don't let him in
Close the door
He doesn't get to write your story anymore.

There is cloud over me tonight
Your shadow without a doubt is there
It lingers in the nights air
To wake up without hesitation
Without a doubt
Why do you blame me?
Tarnish my name
I was a good woman
With too much shame
I stayed after the abuse
Allowed you to cheat
And come and go as you please
All these thoughts they haunt me
Where did my backbone go?
How long did that little girl believe her daddy would come home?
Oh, that's a different story one you would also want to know
My mind I know is still abused
My days are short and lost in a haze
I built my life back within a maze
That one day I would find my way out
Of this place
One day my head won't be the bad place
But like a lost little girl
Who turns to a teen
Opens her legs always at the knees
To let the boys, play while she tries to find peace
Oh, one day I hope you know
You took those legs and spread them apart
I didn't know how to not give you my heart
Now I'm here as my soul bleeds
For that final piece that puts me at ease
The fight you gave me no one knows

But here I am still trying to breathe
Please don't come back
To try and fix what you have broken
I'll sit here and stare at the shadow above me
He is truly the only one who I think still loves me.

I used to find peace in your torture
Like a sinner being punished for an unknown sin
Finally feeling relief
Even if not for the crime they truly committed
Like a child stealing a candy bar
You stole my innocence
Without a thought or hesitation
You took my youth
You took my freedom
You used me as playground for your pleasure
I was nothing to you
Now you ask for empathy and freedom?
You don't want to face the consequences
For your actions
Like the child you stole from me
A part of me died with you
But I am free
To build a life from you
From your sinister ways.

The people in my world
Expect more than I can give
Drain me of my soul
When I'm in the ground don't cry for me
I wish for the truth to prevail
But with the knife to my throat
Breathing is getting harder
The blood dripping is real
I feel peace
But don't cry for me
All your demands and accusations put me there
Your lies that became the truth are what killed me
The fact that none of you know me
Is ok now
I no longer feel the pain
I'm fainting in out of consciousness
I don't regret my choice
Don't be a coward and claim you were there for me
Or you even tried to save me
Don't cry for me
Please confess the truth that made me the liar
Made me scared to tell others anything, don't cry for me
Cause you killed me
The knife is next to me
The blood is pooling
You lost me.

I couldn't see it anymore
It's as if all my future plans stopped
I didn't see us anymore
I just saw me
Again
Alone
Did I fail?
Or am I actually succeeding?
See you came to me
Out of the blue
And I should've never shown you
My darkness, cause that's not what you wanted to see
I found me at one point in my life
Or at least I thought I did
But I lost her again
You gave me my demons back
Looked at me and told me I'm fucked
So now I sit with a choice
Do I fuck myself more and stay?
Or do I walk away again?
Start over, accept me only to face the demons that I ran from
These problems are real
My fear of myself is deep
Who is she actually?
No tears no morals no values
What is she actually capable of?
I don't know she is a third person whom I use
To cover the real, me
The devil in me
This raging war is deep
Who the fuck is she?
Without another one of your kind telling her who to be
Is she really me?

Is my happiness allowed?
Those around me all claim that's what they want to see
But yet here I am
Bleeding internally
I want an array that cheers and roots for me
I want no more envy
I need to learn to control myself
Gossiping does not help
Negativity surrounds me
The lies pile up beneath me
No one speaks nicely
About anyone anymore
I don't want to live in this drama no more
My life will radiate positivity
I will no longer let people around me
Speak poorly about me
I am a good person and I do try
Today I rise above all
Today there's sunshine
And I feel the rays
To help change myself destructive ways.

The pain only stops when you die
For everyone
This isn't just you
The world did not target you
Find me someone who hasn't felt pain
Find me someone who hasn't feared the sunset or dreaded the midnight hour
Find me someone
And I'll believe that we aren't all here to learn
From my understanding the pain is our teacher
Of empathy, compassion and understanding
And that is something we all need to learn
Judging others will not bring us closer.

My writings are dark
My thoughts are the same
This life has me lost
I don't know my purpose
All men treat me the same
They want to make me a wife
So, I'm the one to blame
For the mistake
That after they marry me
Suddenly I'm not the same
I don't understand
Why walk me down an aisle?
Just to cause me pain
My life is just full of me making the same mistake
I should've learned by now
My head is filled with false promises
Long overdue for a day without games
My heart is just an ache
An organ I blame
For allowing me to make the same mistakes.

With a pen and a paper
An ink and a cord
Do you think I hang myself enough?
To let the blood pour
Cause when I cry
All I see is black streaks
Running down my face
Of pure hate and shame
I bear the scars
Hide the truth
But when I look in the mirror
The warrior comes through
Unties the cord from my neck
And reminds me the devil is not done yet.

I play his game oh so well
Moan his name as he drags me down to hell
The orgasm is fierce
The wetness leaks out of me staining my sheets
He knows my body all too well
He feeds off of it on a daily
Cause I guess we all like a little bit of hell
The scorching flames burn my skin
I have him in me
My nails are dragging down his spine
My pussy knows he's all mine
As he drags me back to the place, I know so well
I hope he hears his own screams
And how he calls my name and I cum
I hope he knows
We just made love
Should I tell him it's the devil's drug?

When you first feel the wrenching pain
Your thoughts go back to your happy place
But the sound of his hand across your face always comes back to play
You think you can't take it anymore
Who's really to blame?
Me? For allowing the same mistake
To happen again and again
It's all the fucking same
The next time you fight
You push him just as hard
say the same things as before
Wondering again will he take it that far
To see if he really changed
So, when the replay happens
You don't feel so ashamed
You take responsibility
Is this love real?
If his fist doesn't come at her
Does he even love her?
If her head doesn't smash a few times more
She begs and pleads for it to all end
But she starts the fight to end the end
Again, she's not walking out the door
All because she loved a man with a raging core
No sweetheart that's not love and neither are the whores
A man who loves you doesn't let it get that far
He wouldn't put you through all that and make you beg for more
A man that loves you doesn't want to hurt you
A man that loves you will never leave you pleading for pain to feel something
    more
That's not a man and life's not a game
You can lose it all over a fight about the whore he fucked last night

I know it's hard and you want more
Just to feel like something cause if he fights you back
You must be worth fighting for
This fight will be your last if you open that door.

What is happening to me?
I'm dying inside and can't breathe
My life is at an ultimate low
I don't think I can take another blow
I put my ego aside
And I'm trying to ride it out
See how deep I can go
How many emotions can I feel?
Is this hate real?
Does true love exist?
Or do we just get high on something like it?
And wait for a better fix?
People come and go this much I do know
Whether you push them, or they just walk freely
I know the pain of losing the living
It hurts more than you can imagine
Seeing them breathing.

And I wait
I wait for the attention you claim is there
I want for your hand to find mine again
I long for the stares and kisses
I miss when you used to look at me and wonder why
ask how you got so lucky for me to pick you
Now I just wait
For a rainy day when you want to cuddle
They never come anymore since you're always running out the door
You tell me to be patient
Our time is coming
You're working hard for me aren't you hunny?
Well just so you know
My time is precious too
I used to think nothing was boring with you
Now we sit across from each other
No more romance its long since left the air
It's stale and tense
With resentment and hate
A word I never thought we would both say
All those days we used to waste getting nothing done just a bunch of laughs
    and few poor mistakes
Those were the days we couldn't get enough
Of the touch kiss or gentle caress
Of your hand in mine
Oh, I miss the good old times
So now I wait
To see if this is just another mistake.

When it fades
When it's no longer bright
When that shadow of doubt lingers
And takes the light
That once made you shine
Will you be able to admit the pain then?
Will you still try to hide the shadows that follow you around?
Will you lay there, or will you escape?
Your own demons
Escape your pain
Will you make it out?
Or allow the shadows
To scream out they own you now.

Trying to love me is tiring
I'm wearing myself out
Trying to love me
I'm exhausted
Trying to expect what I give is not what I shall receive
My heart is always crying and aching
Why can't this life be easy?
I try and make different choices
But I keep trying to please all those around me
I'm aching and tired
My head is screaming
My tears are always trying to escape me
This smile is dwindling
And no one is asking me if I'm ok
Can't anybody see?
I'm fucking drowning and screaming
It's all now sinking in
No one will save me
But the world will see I rescued me.

You're trying to stay calm
Keep going to your happy place
But being second has never been your pace
So, you wait patiently trying to keep face
Avoid the yelling, screaming match that's about to take place
You can't stand it anymore
And he can't believe you're acting this way
But nothing is the same in this unfamiliar place
You feel like someone else has taken your space
This lonely feeling is talking
And the voices aren't the same
They are more negative day by day
It's all your fault and you're overreacting
In such a way that you can't control the way you're screaming this time
How would he feel if after all that you tried to build was taken from him?
How will he feel when someone takes his place?
Does he not see this love is becoming a game?
A cat and mouse race
Is he going to react the same?
Give you patience and understanding
Who is he going to blame?
When nothing is the same?
You sweetheart, he'll blame you
Cause after all isn't it your fault that nothing is the same?

I kept your secrets
Held back the truth
Denied all the lies
And never let my lips run loose
I hid my pride
Denied what I felt inside
To keep you by my side
Told everyone it's good
I'm ok
All while keeping a smile on my face
To help hide the disgrace
And shame I had
From knowing the truth
And never letting the secrets go
I know you said you were worth the wait
Life's not a game but you need to win this race
I second guessed and questioned your mistakes
While you screamed in my face
I'm not the same
I don't have your back
And myself is to blame
So, when you're alone
And finish it in first place
Do you think then
Shit between will still be the same?
Or will I have gone insane
Keeping a secret that never parted my lips
That you never really loved me
And I was never really what you wanted
You just didn't want to shame your family name.

That ache, that torture
That familiar pain
That scorching feeling when you're breathing
When you inhale that last breath
That brings you to your knees
That brings you to a place you know all too well
A place you never wanted to be again
All you can do is lay there silently screaming
As the tears roll down your face
As your heart aches that ripping pain
No one is there to pick you up
You're alone going insane
And just as you think you can't bare it anymore
You look up and see his face.

She says go
She wants to be alone
To search for her soul
She lost oh so long ago
The leaves change with time
As she feels like her smile is dwindling from the inside
Her freedom left long ago trapped in hell she shares with not a soul.

Has it changed?
Did you regret it?
Did you leave it?
Did you love it only because you lost it?
Pushing, pulling you're playing tug a war
You got scared and ran away
She won't be what you wanted anymore
But if you leave her
No one else will feel the same
The next one won't fix your pain
You did it to yourself
I have no pity for you
I just feel shame
That I believed in you
And now look, nothing is the same
Just a past between us
Maybe one day I'll be able to say
I was what made you
Until that day I guess I'll keep playing the game
Oh yes, this beautiful game.

The scars, I bare them
My story I shared it
These words are fearing
The truth I told it
The lies I hold them
I face my demon
The one who tried to conquer me
I can't kill it
But I looked him in the eye and told him
I no longer fear it
I swear what almost killed me
Did a little bit
But deep inside I hold onto it
For a reason
To remind me that he no longer owns me
I died some days and some nights I still do
But when this is finished, I will know
I helped kill you
You're welcome
You see I showed you
Some people that bleed should die in peace
And that I give you as my gift
Of pleasure you see
Cause the day you tried to kill me
Was the last time I cared to see you alive
Now die in peace pretty fucking please
There is no me and you
Your grave I do see on a daily
When the dirt hits the top, I'll shed no tear just smile from ear to ear
On that day I'll know I looked peace in the eye
For I will fear no longer of my own demise.

Love is not control
Love is not lies
Love is not pain
Hurt is never disguised as happiness
There is darkness in all of us
It can control
It can turn our directions
It can tell us lies
To change our minds
We have a shield we all carry
Like a woman who builds walls around her heart
We all build walls
With no real idea what we are protecting ourselves from
The story of the gilded girl is a popular one
How her pain carried her forward and pushes her to achieve
But yet it was what ultimately destroyed her because she never fully healed
So, the walls were put up high and go very deep
There has to be a rainbow at the end of all this rain
Just like they all say you will smile again after all this pain.

Does love ever leave?
The person may leave
You no longer see them
Feel their lingering stare
No longer pain when you see their smile
The person may leave
Love though, true love never leaves
Love may fade and distance and time make it all easier to bare
Memories will flash on rare occasions
With a reminder that there once was something there
How you feel from then to now
Has increasingly changed
It's hard to bury pain
Of the dead that still remain
Something so simple will remind you of that pain
And how you wish to never go back to the good old days
Today you stay strong and free
With the haunting memory
That love never leaves.

Confused and in a daze
The snow fell around her
You could see her eyes turn to a glaze
As memories flashed from past days
It's the reason to bring back the pain
I'll never know why this happens
I start to wonder will the memories go away
The loneliness
The haze
The questions
It's a puzzle inside of a maze
'Tis the season I keep saying
Her eyes are still a glaze
I wonder again as I push the memory away
Will this ever change
The question still lingers in the winters air
The answers will never be there because your love may be true but his was
    never there.

I have made choices that hurt
I have made some that felt right
I have stayed up late wishing to see the sunrise
Not only cause my nightmares haunt me
But to see the true beauty of the sun peaking
Some nights those choices and those feelings drive me fucking crazy
I live for the future so I'm always in a panic
Of the next choice I'll have to make
And I wonder if this one is going to cause more damage
I live with the regret of some of my dreams
Only living cause, they haunt me in my sleep
I pray daily for some sanity
But everyday there is less clarity
I live with the notion this too shall pass
Only to feel nothing while my days pass
I want my nightmares to end now please
So maybe I won't make the same choices that haunt me in my sleep.

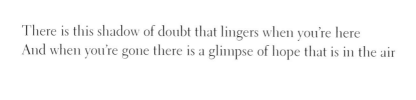

There is this shadow of doubt that lingers when you're here
And when you're gone there is a glimpse of hope that is in the air

There was a knock at the door dressed in sin
She opened the door and let him in
Blinded by his beauty her eternity was his
He was devil and her soul now for him
But all his beauty was only the outside
She didn't realize that was his disguise
He will be all consuming
Cause he only has one thought in mind
So as you feel the floor crumble beneath you
As you feel like running his flames will be all captivating
You'll try to leave I know you will
But sweetheart it's way too late
He will have you thinking it's a big mistake
He will break you down but leave you wanting more
And no one can save you
Cause when the devil came knocking you opened the door.

Here we go again
Same mistake
Different time
I give my all
And expect the same
I run and hide and cry
You lie and lie
And have more lies
My emotions are blocked
I'm ashamed of who I am inside

Printed in the United States
By Bookmasters